AQUARIUMS
FOR YOUR NEW PET

MARY ELLEN SWEENEY

CONTENTS

Photographs by Dr. Herbert R. Axelrod, B. Kahl, H.-J. Richter, A. Roth, K. Knaack, S. Frank, L. Wischnath, R. Zukal, J. Palicka and Cole Enterprises.
Illustrations by J. R. Quinn.

Inside front cover: Pearl gourami. Inside back cover: *Melanotaenia goldiei.*

9 8 7 6 5 4 3 2 1   **1995 Edition**   9 6789

Distributed in the UNITED STATES to the Pet Trade by T.F.H. Publications, Inc., One T.F.H. Plaza, Neptune City, NJ 07753; distributed in the UNITED STATES to the Bookstore and Library Trade by National Book Network, Inc. 4720 Boston Way, Lanham MD 20706; in CANADA to the Pet Trade by H & L Pet Supplies Inc., 27 Kingston Crescent, Kitchener, Ontario N2B 2T6; Rolf C. Hagen Ltd., 3225 Sartelon Street, Montreal 382 Quebec; in CANADA to the Book Trade by Vanwell Publishing Ltd., 1 Northrup Crescent, St. Catharines, Ontario L2M 6P5 ; in ENGLAND by T.F.H. Publications, PO Box 15, Waterlooville PO7 6BQ; in AUSTRALIA AND THE SOUTH PACIFIC by T.F.H. (Australia), Pty. Ltd., Box 149, Brookvale 2100 N.S.W., Australia; in NEW ZEALAND by Brooklands Aquarium Ltd. 5 McGiven Drive, New Plymouth, RD1 New Zealand; in Japan by T.F.H. Publications, Japan—Jiro Tsuda, 10-12-3 Ohjidai, Sakura, Chiba 285, Japan; in SOUTH AFRICA by Lopis (Pty) Ltd., P.O. Box 39127, Booysens, 2016, Johannesburg, South Africa. Published by T.F.H. Publications, Inc.

MANUFACTURED IN THE UNITED STATES OF AMERICA
BY T.F.H. PUBLICATIONS, INC.

CHOOSING YOUR EQUIPMENT

There are many good reasons to keep tropical fishes: an interest in plant and animal life, the desire to have some living creatures in your home, maybe the need for a relaxing hobby to soothe you after the day's work. Whatever your reason, there can be no doubt that once you have started with tropical fish, you will have an enchanting hobby that will give you tremendous pleasure for years to come.

There are many advantages to keeping tropical fishes as pets. They can easily be kept in the smallest apartment. Even the most adamant landlord would hardly be likely to object to them on the basis of a "No Pets" clause in your lease. They don't need to be walked or groomed and they won't disturb the neighbors. Some people, who for health reasons thought that they could never keep a pet,

A beautiful, well-planted and well-stocked community tank pleases both the eye and the spirit.

are delighted to find that they can have as many aquariums as they wish.

Whether your motivation for starting an aquarium is the love of nature or the desire to reproduce a small bit of a tropical stream in your home, I am sure that you will learn something about your fishes every day.

Tanks

There are many different types of aquariums that you can set up. The purpose of this book is to introduce you to the tropical fishes. Not all aquariums contain tropical fishes. There are coldwater aquariums that house goldfish, koi and other non-tropical species. There are also marine tanks, minireefs, invertebrate tanks, brackish tanks, and more. There is almost unlimited variety in the fishkeeping hobby.

Taking first things first, you will need a tank. That sounds simple, but you will find any number of variables even in the selection of a basic vessel for the containment of the objects of your new hobby. The traditional fish tank was a rectangular glass box with a metal frame. If this is your only conception of an aquarium, you

This unusually shaped aquarium is possible because of the recent use of acrylics by aquarium manufacturers. Notice, however, that there are not many fishes in this tank. Such a design requires that you choose your pets carefully and do not overstock with fishes.

are in for a pleasant surprise…and a great number of possible choices. Aquaria are constructed as rectangles, hexagons, octagons, tall cylinders, desk-top aquariums, domes, bubbles, even coffee tables. Of course, you could put your fish in just about anything that is clean and holds water. I kept some common goldfish for a summer in an old-fashioned porcelain wash basin in our cellar. They got enormous.

Little did I know at the age of eleven that I was also culturing the live food (mosquitoes) responsible for these gargantuans. Fishes are kept in ponds, glass bowls, mayonnaise jars, and even brandy snifters. The possibilities can boggle the imagination. Mostly, though, you want your fishes housed in a tank that affords a pleasing view and is compatible with their well-being.

Whether you decide on a 5-gallon acrylic, desk-top model or a 100-gallon giant, you will want the tank to hold water, so buy the highest quality aquarium your budget will allow. If it is a large tank (30 gallons or more), the glass will need to be at least 6 mm thick with proportionally thicker or cast glass on the bottom. Refuse a tank with deep scratches, especially on the long sides or bottom. The silicone on the seams should be evenly distributed and free from blobs or gaps.

The size of the aquarium you select depends to a large extent upon the species, size, and number of fishes you wish to house. However, the shape of the tank also has a great deal to do with what types of fishes can be housed within. A tall thin cylinder is naturally a more limiting environment than a tank that is shallow and has a large surface area for gaseous exchange. That is not to say that you can't successfully have the fascinating, decorative work of living art in some of the more unusually shaped aquariums. You just have to compensate in some way when the surface area isn't very large. This is often accomplished by the movement of the water with pumps and airstones.

If we are setting up an aquarium for bettas, for example, it would not be a great big deal to use one of the tall cylinders with very little surface area, as bettas are labyrinth fishes, having the ability to utilize atmospheric oxygen, and, therefore, need less oxygenated water. But this is not the norm. It is best to purchase your tank armed with knowledge and common sense.

Virtually every aquarist counsels, "Buy the largest tank you can afford." The reason for this oft-repeated advice is not fishkeeper's snobbery. It is practical and truly to your benefit because a larger body of water is much more forgiving of environmental contaminants (such as hair spray, smoke, and

These are some of the more conventional aquarium designs. Most companies also manufacture compatible stands for their aquariums.

fumes of many kinds), changes in water temperature, and myriad other factors that could prove hazardous to your "finny" population…and you can keep more fishes. I don't personally know of anyone who can resist the urge to "add just one more." Well, in a 10-gallon aquarium, that urge is soon contained—or else! Please understand that I am not, nor would I ever denigrate the trusty old 10-gallon jobber. (How well I remember the thrill of graduating from a fish-murdering bowl to a gigantic (10-gallon "real" aquarium!) Five- and 10-gallon tanks definitely have their place, when used intelligently, within our hobby. Smaller tanks are excellent for fry, breeding pairs, a few small fishes, and those of us who otherwise could not have an aquarium, and those few people (of a different species from the rest of us) who can hold the population down to a reasonable size. Because, believe me, if you don't keep the population appropriate to the tank, Mother Nature will do it for you…and the fish you lose may just be your favorite. Just remember, the smaller the tank, the better an aquarist you must be.

The aquarium must have a stable surface to rest upon. There are many commercially-made aquarium stands. As long as the stand is strong, stable, and places the aquarium at a comfortable viewing height, it will do the job. Remember that water weighs approximately 8 pounds per gallon. Include the gravel, tank, and other accessories, and your average 10-gallon tank weighs over 100 pounds. What this means is that

you are going to have to be very sure that the stand will accommodate the load. That's why your best bet is to buy an appropriate stand from your pet shop.

When you place the tank on the stand, it's advisable to put a piece of styrofoam, felt, or other thin cushion between the tank and the stand to alleviate any stress caused by a slight unevenness that could cause the glass to break.

Although it is highly improbable that your floor will not be able to support this load, take note also of the condition of the floor. If you live in a very old house and the floor is not as stable as it could be, consider placing a very large aquarium over the supporting joists, just to be on the safe side.

Filters

Your filter will have a great deal to do with the success or failure of this new hobby of yours, so it is very important that you get the best filter for the set-up you are planning. The filtration system will perform a number of functions in your aquarium. Quite simply, the water is forced through some type of filtering media, usually synthetic floss and charcoal. There are many other types of filtering media, of course: sand, sponge, ceramic "macaroni," and even the gravel itself as in the undergravel filter.

The action of the water through the filter media helps to remove particulate matter, such as uneaten food, fish wastes, and suspended algae. Filtration is also very useful in circulating the water, which is necessary for the exchange of oxygen and carbon dioxide. Even though your fishes live underwater and usually don't breathe oxygen as we do from the air, they still need oxygen for respiration. Water that is

The young man in the photo has installed a piece of felt between aquarium and stand for safety.

of disturbing the fishes. Also, one of the goals of filtration is the development of beneficial bacterial colonies that break down harmful wastes (ammonia) into less harmful nitrates. These colonies, if constantly disturbed, cannot do an adequate job. However, box filters are still great for small- to medium-sized, sparsely populated tanks, and the box can be attractively disguised by plants.

The outside power filter is very convenient and easy to use. It is also a splendid vehicle for the desirable biological activity. With this type of filter we have a box and pump in one unit. The box containing the filter media hangs on the back side of the aquarium, and the only portion that goes into the aquarium is the water intake tube. The water goes up into the filter, passes through the filter media where the particles are trapped, and then, cleaned and aerated, pours

deficient in oxygen will soon have fishes gasping at the surface, trying to breathe.

The most commonly used filter is probably still the inside box filter. But there are some drawbacks with this filter type. If one has a large aquarium, it would require several of these filters to adequately clear the water. This would be undesirable because of the room they would take up in the tank. Also, this type of filter needs to be cleaned rather frequently and involves a certain amount of mess and disturbance of the aquarium decor…to say nothing

or is pumped back into the tank. When the water passes through the filter media, it is "treated" by the microscopic bacteria residing therein and returns to the tank in a much more healthful condition. The flow rate of the water passing through this type of filter can be controlled by the aquarist, even to turning it off at feeding time so the food is not wasted by being drawn into the filter.

The undergravel filter is probably the ultimate as far as biological filtration goes, since most of the work of this type of filter is performed by bacteria. However, an undergravel filter does a poor job of removing particles from the water and should be used in conjunction with some other type of filter. An undergravel filter is just what it sounds like. The filter plate is placed under the gravel bed, leaving about a quarter-inch gap between the filter plate and the bottom of the aquarium. The slotted plastic plate is fitted with airlift tubes that reach the top of the aquarium. The tubes pull to the surface the cleaned water which is constantly being replaced by water drawn down through the gravel and filter plate. The water being sucked down through the gravel is filtered partly by the gravel

itself and also by the bacteria bed flourishing undisturbed beneath the undergravel filter. The primary action employed by the undergravel filter is biological filtration which, in conjunction with your regular partial water changes, will keep the toxic wastes from building up in the tank and killing all life within.

There are also canister filters, sponge filters, wet/dry filters and many more types appearing on the scene regularly. The

One type of filter is an internal canister filter, which can be put right into the tank, with both pump and filtering areas being completely submerged. Photo courtesy of Hagen.

9

canister filter is the real workhorse of aquarium filtration. Used primarily for larger aquaria, the canister filter employs multiple layers of filtering media for a combination of biological and mechanical filtration. No matter which type filter you select, the basic principle remains the same. The water goes in dirty at one end and comes out clean at the other. Any one or more of these systems will go a long way toward helping you maintain the optimal water conditions so desirable for a clean, sparkling aquarium full of healthy fish.

The Nitrogen Cycle

Biological filtration is not quite as mysterious as it may sound. This is the process whereby the invisible, colorless poisons (ammonia and nitrite) are rendered harmless by bacterial action. Ammonia is the main toxic material produced as fish waste and by the decomposition of leftover food. When your filter is working properly, and has had time to establish itself, it is the home of colonies of beneficial bacteria called *Nitrosomonas.* The bacteria convert the ammonia to a less harmful material, called nitrite. After the toxic ammonia is converted to the less toxic, but by no means "safe" nitrite, another bacterium, *Nitrobacter* (which also flourishes in an established filter), goes to work and converts the nitrite into the relatively benign compound, nitrate. The nitrogen cycle is an integral facet of every successful aquarium. The establishment of this cycle takes a little time. One of the fundamental strategies in setting up your aquarium is to do so slowly, adding very few fish and plants at first, and then as the biological activity becomes more established, reaching full population. There are products

on the market that will help reduce the waiting period, however, by allowing you to introduce started colonies of these bacteria and help to establish the nitrogen cycle more quickly.

However, since ammonia, nitrite, and nitrate are only part of the waste being produced in a living, breathing, reproducing, and excreting aquarium, you cannot expect the bacteria to do all the work for you. You still must change part of the water regularly and keep an eye on the condition of the filter media and change it when necessary.

Lighting

Usually the lighting fixture and tank hood come as one unit, making for a convenient arrangement. Part of the hood raises for easy access to the aquarium for feeding and maintenance, and the light switch is right there close at hand. While many tank covers are still equipped for

incandescent bulbs, it is much better, for the sake of both fish and plants, to get one that uses fluorescent tubes. Fluorescent tubes, while slightly more expensive at the outset, burn longer and cooler than incandescent ones. It is important that the water is not overheated by the light source, as it can be with incandescent bulbs. "Good," you may be thinking, "I'll just get incandescent bulbs and then I won't have to buy a heater." Sorry. First, you won't be able

to control the amount of heat given off by the bulbs. It may not even be enough to warm the water sufficiently. Second, the heat will be concentrated in the top level of the water, leaving cold pockets below that will serve neither flora nor fauna.

For the benefit of both plants and fish, it is best to keep the lighting on a regular schedule. Twelve to 14 hours of illumination a day have been found to be most effective. The light can even be on a timer if you desire, so the timer could turn on the light in the afternoon when you're at work or school; then you have the enjoyment of your aquarium in the evening without becoming a slave to the lighting schedule. Also, when installing your light,

the bulb should be placed toward the front of the tank to create more depth of field and enhance your view of the fishes.

For beautiful plants, choose a warm-toned fluorescent bulb concentrating its intensity at both the blue and red ends of the spectrum. Additionally, your plants will also do much better if your cover is equipped with a reflector.

Heaters and Thermometers

When keeping tropicals, you will definitely want to be able to accurately control the temperature of the water. Many of the ailments that afflict fish can be directly attributed to extreme changes in water temperature. One of the best things you can do for yourself

There are many types of thermometers to determine the temperature of your aquarium water, including floating, stick-on with suction cup and digital. Photos courtesy of Hagen.

in your new hobby is to purchase a good heater and thermometer.

For my money, the thermometer of choice is the heat-sensitive liquid crystal type, which is attached directly to the glass, unlike the floating bulb type that is always bobbing around and never where you want it to be. I usually like to put the thermometer on the side glass, where it is easily read but doesn't obstruct the front view. Even though many heaters have built-in thermostats, which are very convenient, it is still good to be able to check a thermometer for accuracy. It is not unheard of for a heater element to stick and overheat the water.

Probably the most popular heater is one where the heater and thermostat are combined. These heaters automatically maintain the pre-set temperature in the aquarium within a couple of degrees either way. (*Minor gradual fluctuations in temperature aren't going to hurt any but the most sensitive or sickly fish.*)

When working with your tank, make sure you don't leave the heater on when emptying the tank or plug in a dry heater. This could cause the glass tube to crack and ruin the heater.

Also, don't put a hot heater into water. Unplug the heater, let it cool, then put it in the water and plug it in again.

Air Pumps

The usual aerator is an electric pump. In the old days, pumps were noisy and troublesome. Modern engineering has produced pumps that are virtually silent and maintenance-free. They are inexpensive to operate in terms of energy cost. Pumps are usually operated by a vibrating diaphragm, which is preferred over piston pumps. They do not

Vibrator air pumps vary in size and the amount of air they can produce, but they all share in one very attractive feature in comparison to the older-style piston pumps: they require far less electrical power for their operation. Photo courtesy of Hagen.

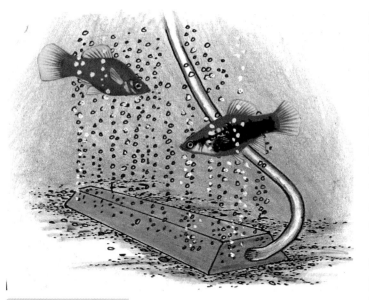

increasing the exchange of oxygen and carbon dioxide at the surface of the water. Not much oxygen is absorbed by the water from the air pumped through the airstone, but the extra movement at the water's surface does have a beneficial effect on the oxygen level of the water. A medium-sized spray of bubbles is more efficient than either large or small bubbles.

Change the inexpensive airstones fairly often as the pores can clog and this will cause back-up pressure that can damage the pump.

Several airstones and filters can be run from the same pump by using a very simple gang-valve device.

Aquarium Decor

There is an unbelievable assortment of accessories that enhance the decor of your fishes' watery home. Purists believe that the only way to decorate an aquarium is with the natural scenery that the collector would discover while seeking the specimens in the wild. Balderdash, I say! If you want red gravel and a burping fluorescent clam, go for it. But be prepared to defend yourself. (Don't call me, I've got other fish to fry.)

The first item on your agenda

Airstones complement your filtration and assist in the circulation of the water column in the aquarium. They are inexpensive and a good investment.

require oiling and are very quiet. Piston pumps do have better output, though.

The pump should be placed above the level of the water to prevent water backing into it through the airline when the plug is pulled.

Or use check valves available in pet shops.

Airstones

The tiny bubbles you see in your dealer's tanks are made possible by airstones. These airstones are very inexpensive and easy to come by. Air from a pump is forced through the porous "stone." The purpose of the airstone is to increase both the surface movement of the water and the circulation of the water within the tank, thus

will be the substrate. Substrate is the correct term for the "floor" of your biotope. According to the *American Heritage Dictionary,* a *biotope* is a "… limited ecological region or niche in which the environment is suitable for certain forms of life." So when choosing your substrate, you must bear in mind that this element will contribute to the biotope as a whole. There's the old standby, colored gravel; it's uniform in size, sold in a broad range of colors, cheap, usually inoffensive; it is boring. Why not choose to approximate the real, or at least possible, natural biotope? I say "approximate" the biotope because it would be difficult, if not downright impossible, to create a genuine facsimile stream or riverbed in the limited space available in even the largest tank in a public aquarium. Besides, it wouldn't be worth the effort. The real decor of the natural environment could just as easily include an old tire as an esthetically pleasing piece of striated rock. So what we'll do is take the best and leave the rest.

The substrate serves a variety of functions. It covers the bottom of the tank. It covers the undergravel filter and creates the filter bed. It anchors and contains nutrients for your plants. It is attractive. It gives the fish an occupation. The bottom-feeders and earth-movers utilize the bottom layer in many of their daily activities. Part of the fascination of watching some species is observing how they will patiently move the gravel around to suit themselves, sometimes digging a hole, sometimes building a little hill.

The size of the particles of your substrate should be about 2 to 6 mm. A neutral color is more pleasing to the fish than white or light-colored materials. The darker colors also have the benefit of not showing the dirt. The substrate must be clean and free of debris or chemicals. For the most part, one can assume that commercially available gravels are not hazardous to the fishes. The gravel will, however, probably be quite dirty and needs to be rinsed

An established aquarium will support many plants. The rock is useful to anchor the plants around it.

15

several times, until the water runs clear, to remove dust and odd particles.

Except when specializing in grubbing fishes like catfish, loaches, barbs, some dwarf cichlids, etc., avoid fine sand as it gets muddy quickly, aerates poorly, and thus is generally unacceptable. When the small pores of fine sand get clogged with debris, the plant roots can't get any oxygen and the plant will perish. Coarser natural-colored pebbles are very attractive and functional, but even with these there could be problems for certain brooding fishes who care for their babies if the fry or eggs fall between the cracks and can't get out.

It seems that one of the best substrates is a combination of coarse and finer pebbles. Trapped food doesn't accumulate and rot, and fry have a chance at life.

Rockwork is important to many fishes and can certainly provide interesting and useful aquarium decorations. For the most part, stay away from marble, shells, and corals when keeping freshwater tropical fishes. It is not worth the risk unless you are absolutely certain that they are safe. The types of rocks suitable for freshwater are granite, basalt, and sandstone. Rocks and stones should not have sharp edges that could injure the fishes. Many fish choose flat stones as their spawning sites and will stubbornly refuse romance unless they have these. Large stones can lead to stress cracks in the glass. Just be sure there is no chance of your rock structure collapsing, since even a fairly small rock can break the glass or kill an unfortunate fish. Rocks can be silicone-cemented to each other for extra security, but it is difficult to change the arrangement once this is done. Any rock you choose to use must be well-washed first. You pet shop has an attractive assortment of aquarium decorations; this should be your source for anything you use inside your tank.

Driftwood is often included in the aquarium and is very interesting, giving your fishes additional places to explore, create territories in, and hide when necessary. The fishes in your tank are definitely more interesting to watch when they have objects to navigate around, above, below, or through. It is best to avoid the temptation to overcrowd the tank with too many things, though, as this could cause a maintenance problem. You will need access to the substrate from time to time. There will be times you will want to catch a fish or two, and this could prove quite a challenge if there are too many hiding places.

If you bought your driftwood from a pet shop, usually the only thing you need to do before putting it in your aquarium is to wash it with hot water. If, however, you just stumbled on this great piece of wood on a lakeside stroll, then there are a few things you must know before its inclusion into the tank. Dead tree roots that have been underwater for quite a while are generally ideal, as are petrified woods. It is not a good idea to use freshly cut wood since there are saps, resins and other undesirable components involved. If you do find a nice piece of wood (not too large, though; it doesn't take much to overpower an aquarium), boil it before you include it in your decor. If it is buoyant, lead anchors will keep it down, or you could silicone it to the bottom or rear wall of the aquarium.

Bamboo reeds are also used for a somewhat different effect and can be very nice in one corner for a vertical arrangement. The main thing to keep in mind is that anything you put into your tank must be absolutely clean. It would not be overcautious to boil anything you are going to put in your aquarium (except for the living things, of course).

The theme of your aquatic landscape must be balance. It is very tempting to go overboard with the various decorative items you could cram the tank with, perhaps believing you will have better "luck" with your hobby. There is no voodoo in the artistic arrangement of the aquarium. Divers and mermaids are no substitute for sound aquarium management. So, when designing the interior of your tank, leave ample free space. This is important for the visual beauty as well as for the welfare of your fishes.

Swordtails and angelfish are not the best choice as tankmates. As the cute little angels mature, they will become more aggressive, and when the time comes for romance, all their tankmates will be harassed by their jealous guarding of their mate and eggs.

17

SETTING UP THE AQUARIUM

A good start promises a good result. I doubt that there are many endeavors where this is more true than in dealing with the aquarium hobby. After purchasing the essential equipment, we are ready to set up the tank, decorate, and add water. Remember, buy no fishes at this point! We want this new hobby of yours to get off on the right fin.

First, choose a location. For the most part, it is better to keep the tank away from a window. There are too many things that can go wrong: temperature fluctuations, rampant algae growth, and too much light. Selection of the proper location will give you maximum control over the effects of the outdoor world on your indoor water world. When positioning your aquarium, also be sure you put it close to an electrical outlet. It's probably wise to invest in some multi-plug receptors, because aquarists never seem to have enough electrical outlets. Please be careful—the combination of electricity and water can be extremely hazardous to your health. Ground-fault circuit breakers are highly recommended!

Set your stand in the chosen location (bearing in mind that you won't want to move the tank once it has been filled with water). Next, take the tank to the tub or outside with a garden hose and rinse well. We never know what contaminant may have been deposited on the glass during transit. Even dust will make the water cloudy if there's enough of it. Some people advocate washing the tank with salt and rinsing well just to be on the safe side, and this is strongly recommended if the tank has been used before. NEVER, EVER, USE SOAP ON ANY TANK! (This also goes for nets, filters, and other aquarium equipment.) Don't actually fill the tank at this time. You're just giving it a wash. Check for leaks. If you have sprung a leak, the tank can be returned to the reputable dealer who sold it, or easily repaired

Wash the gravel thoroughly before you introduce it to the aquarium.

with silicone on the inside seam. Just follow the directions provided with the silicone. Place the tank on the stand with a pad beneath it.

The gravel must be washed well. Even high quality commercial gravel will contain dust and a certain amount of debris. The easiest way is to put the gravel in a bucket or colander and run water through it, stirring, until the water runs clear. This may take some time, but the cleaner the gravel, the sooner the water in the tank will "settle down" and become clear. After the gravel is well-rinsed, gently pour it into the tank.

Place your decorative pieces before you add the water. Then you can move them around as much as you like and you won't even get your elbows wet.

19

Sloping the gravel towards the back of the tank gives the illusion of more depth and makes cleaning easier because detritus (fish and tank waste, also called mulm) will collect at the front of the tank, where you can remove it easily with the siphon.

With the tank empty of water, decorate. Experiment until you find a look you like. Remember, you will not be able to use live plants at this point, so a few

nice plastic specimens will do a lot for the look of the new tank.

Now you can place a bowl on the gravel and gently pour the lukewarm water into the bowl. Using a bowl will prevent the stream of water from disrupting your decor. Don't fill the tank all the way to the top, as you may want to make adjustments; you can top it off later when everything is in its final place.

The filter can be installed now. Read the manufacturer's instructions for the correct way to operate the filter. There are minor variations in the operation of different filters, but each will use some type of filter media.

If yours uses charcoal separately, rinse the charcoal well before putting it in the filter. Plug the filter or pump in and you should be able to see it working in a moment. Most of the outside power filters need to be primed with some water to operate, but this information will also be included in the packaging. As with most appliances, there will be instructions and warranties. Save this information! It will surely be very valuable to you in time.

Install the heater, leaving it unplugged for a short time so the glass can adjust to the temperature of the water, then set for the desired temperature. Most heaters have a "pilot" light that will come on when the heater is working. Usually a rear or unobtrusive side wall is the best place for the filter and heater, just as long as it's easy to access for maintenance. It will take some time for the heater to achieve the correct temperature in a new tank. Remember, never take the heater out of water while it's on. Unplug it first. Also, do not put a hot heater in cool water. The thermometer can easily be installed, either on the outside of the glass or in the tank, depending on which type you have chosen. Check the temperature. You will be able to tell in a few hours that the heater is indeed doing its job.

Your heater is very easily installed on a the back or side glass of the aquarium.

If you are using an airstone, or several, simply attach the airstone to the pump with an airline and insert the stone in an unobtrusive spot. There are some long stones designed to aerate the whole back of the aquarium, and these are easily set against the back wall on top of the gravel.

Set the hood unit on top of the tank and survey your work. This is the time to make your adjustments. Are the airlines secure? There are no leaks in the seams of the tank? Is the filter working? You should be able to see movement of the water and bubbles. Guide the wires neatly to their plug. Some people use electrical tape to secure the wires and airlines to the tank stand. Loose wires and tubing give even the nicest tank a sloppy, unkempt look. If everything in the tank is working fine, top off the water, check and adjust the pH, add chlorine remover, and you should be able to add some fish to the tank in a few days (a four-day wait is recommended). I suggest that you buy inexpensive, hardy fish at first.

Do not be alarmed if your lovely new aquarium turns cloudy a day or so after you've added your stock. This is not uncommon and is a sign of the new biological activity. This "new tank syndrome" will not be alleviated by a water change. The introduction of bacterial cultures when setting up the tank will minimize it, but probably won't eliminate the cloudiness entirely. Don't despair! As long as you feed lightly and haven't tried to put too many fishes in a new tank, the water will clear spontaneously in a few days.

Water Quality

Much has been said about water quality, but what is it and how do I get it? There are several factors involved in the

quality of your water: pH,
hardness, chlorine, chloramine,
ammonia, nitrites and nitrates,
and even salinity comes into the
picture in some tanks. You may
have a water supply that has the
exact correct conditions for the
fish you wish to keep, but this is
often not the case. However,
there are many products that
will assist the aquarist in
maintaining optimal water
conditions. Your pet shop will
be intimately associated with
the exact nature of the water in
your municipality and will
probably be able to advise you
if any treatment is indeed
necessary. The chlorine and
chloramines that are usually
added to our municipal water
supplies can easily be
neutralized a few drops of
chlorine/chloramine remover
according to manufacturer's
instructions. Hard water is
usually alkaline; soft water is
usually neutral to acid in
reaction. Acidity and alkalinity
are measured on a scale which
goes from 0 to 14 and is called
the pH scale. Neutral water has
a pH of 7 while acid water is
less and alkaline water is more.
Most fishes are very
comfortable with the pH within
1 or 2 degrees of neutral, but
there are the exceptions. Good
aquarium literature will cite
water values for the individual
species and this will guide you.

The water test kits are very
useful in giving the aquarist the
necessary information to help
maintain proper water
conditions. The tests involve
chemical treatment of a small
water sample which will reveal
pH, nitrites, hardness, ammonia
levels, etc., depending on the
test. Then these values can be
adjusted to ideal with the
correct solution, often provided
with the test kit. With an acid
pH or high nitrate and ammonia
levels, though, usually the
culprit is not the chemistry of
the water as such, but rather the
uncleanliness of the water.
When these levels are out of
sync, it's time for a water
change.

SELECTION OF FISHES

Now that your aquarium has been set up a while (72 hours at least), the water is clear, the pH is between 6.8 and 7.2, the temperature is 75 to 80°F, and the filter is chugging merrily away, it's the hour we have all been waiting for. Time to go buy the fish!

One of the most delightful aspects of the aquarium hobby is choosing the fishes you want to keep. And probably one of the most often asked questions in the pet shop is, "Will these fish get along with the ones I already have at home?" The compatibility of your selections is perhaps the most important factor of your decisions. Generally speaking, if they are about the same size, have the same requirements for water parameters, and are not aggressive, they should be able to coexist peacefully. This is very general. For example, some fishes are peaceful no matter what their size, like the pearl gourami *(Trichogaster leeri)*. A pearl gourami virtually never nips a fin. A pearl gourami will, however, eat a very small fish. One must realize that in nature fishes eat other fishes. That is how things

work. They also eat plants, worms, and even their own fry. So it behooves one not to try to

A stunning pearl gourami, *Trichogaster leeri*, builds a bubblenest to receive the female's eggs.

combine even peaceful fishes with other fishes small enough to be overtaken and eaten. On the other hand, there are some species that are well known for their aggressiveness. Some

Cichlasoma managuense is one tough cichlid and requires a large tank with plenty of rocky territories.

cichlids are such terrors that they cannot even be combined with others of their own kind, like *Cichlasoma managuense.* Yet, there are many people who are fascinated with these fishes and delight in their habits.

Certain fishes are better suited to the community tank than others. The distinction may be due to conditional preference, size, breeding habits, feeding requirements, or temperament. For example, one would not want to put a guppy in the same tank with an oscar *(Astronotus ocellatus),* unless the guppy was purchased for the specific purpose of feeding the oscar.

For a balanced look to your tank, you will probably want to include fishes that occupy different levels. One of the ways to tell where you will find the fish is to look at its mouth.

Astronotus ocellatus, the oscar, is a large cichlid with a personality and intelligence to match its size.

Usually if the mouth is turned up, the fish will stay close to the top. A fish whose mouth is in the middle will stay around the center of the tank, and bottom dwellers' mouths are turned down. A fish's mouth is also a pretty accurate indicator of how it will get along with its tankmates … a fish with a large mouth usually has a large appetite and no conscience.

There are essentially five groups of fishes from which you may choose when populating a community aquarium: livebearers, schooling fishes, bottom dwellers, anabantoids, and some cichlids. Of course, there are many more types of fishes, but species from these five groups are the best for the beginner. Each group has the distinction of being relatively easy to maintain, accepting a wide range of water conditions, and eating almost anything. Also, these fishes are comparatively non-aggressive and inexpensive. Any of these fishes can be kept together with a few notable exceptions (more than one male betta per tank and many cichlids, for example), or you can forget the community aspect and set up what is called a "species tank," where all the occupants are the same. Species

Tiny cardinal tetras grace this well-planted aquarium.

The guppy, or millions fish, *Poecilia reticulata*.

tanks are also lovely when you are using relatively small schooling fish, like the cardinal tetras *(Paracheirodon axelrodi)*, which create a moving mass of vibrant color, changing direction in unison for no apparent reason.

Livebearers are probably the most popular fishes for beginners. They give birth to free-swimming young that are self-sufficient when born. They are also considered fair game by every adult fish in the tank (including their own parents), and have to be protected in some way. The most common livebearers are guppies *Poecilia reticulata)*, platies *Xiphophorus* spp.) swordtails

(Xiphorhorus helleri), and black mollies *(Poecilia sphenops)*. Because of the long, flowing tails of most male guppies, it is not advisable to put them in with some of the more nippy species, like some of the barbs. There are almost endless varieties of these fishes, with new ones being developed almost daily.

The term "schooling fish" is an artificial grouping that contains many different types of fishes, but all of them swim together in schools if there are enough of them. Most of these fishes are egglayers. It would be unusual for these fishes to reproduce in a community tank and have any of the fry survive.

remain small enough to be perfect for the community aquarium.

Bottom-dwellers are recommended for just about every aquarium. They are rarely troublesome to their tankmates and perform vital functions—namely scavenging the substrate for leftover food and moving the gravel about a bit which helps keep it tidy. This does not mean that you should offer only

When buying fishes that school, it is desirable to purchase at least six to eight individuals or they will not fully exhibit their schooling behavior. The major types of fishes that can be included in this category are: tetras *(Paracheirodon, Hyphessobrycon,* and *Hemigrammus* spp.), barbs *(Puntius, Barbodes,* and *Capoeta* spp.), danios *(Brachydanio* and *Danio* spp.), and the rainbowfishes *(Melanotaenia* spp.). Most of the fishes in this group will

leftovers to your cats and loaches, but they will help remove food that would otherwise foul the water. There are many, many species and just about each one has something to endear it to the hobbyist. There are catfishes *(Corydoras* spp.), spiny eels, *(Mastacembelus* spp.), loaches, *(Botia* spp.) and some kinds of "sharks," *(Labeo* spp.). Catfishes of the genus *Corydoras* are familiar aquarium residents and very

peaceful. There is another catfish type, known as *Hypostomus plecostomus,* that is always good for a comment, beautiful in its ugliness. Loaches are also very interesting and peaceful. The weather loach in particular is reputed to be an accurate forecaster of barometric changes—abandoning its usual station on the aquarium floor and swimming up and down constantly. Snake-like in appearance, it can also be seen "hanging out" in a favorite plant. The coolie loach and the clown loach are also very attractive and interesting tenants.

Anabantoids are commonly known as labyrinth fishes, which means they have an accessory breathing organ that permits them to extract oxygen from the air. Do not misinterpret this to mean they can live on land—but they can "breathe" air from the surface of the water when conditions below aren't exactly favorable. There are three types of anabantoids: 1) paradisefishes, 2) bettas, 3) gouramis. Paradisefishes were one of the first types of tropical fishes to be kept in the home aquarium. Only a single pair of these fish should be kept in a community tank.

Betta splendens, better known as the Siamese fighting fish, is one of the most popular aquarium fishes because of its

rich red, blue, purple or combined coloring. However, the males are very aggressive among themselves and cannot be kept together under any circumstances. One male may be kept with several females, however. There are several species of *Betta* available to the hobbyist and any one of them would be a good communal aquarium fish. Be sure though, as with the guppy, that their gorgeous fins are not at risk from their tankmates.

Gouramis are lovely

aquarium fishes. They are mild-mannered and have lovely colors. Some of them can grow quite large, though, so it is best to check first if you have a small tank. *Colisa* spp. stay within tolerable size, the largest being about 2 or 3 inches. Some of the *Trichogaster* spp. can grow to about 6 inches and therefore would require quite large quarters. Any of the anabantoids will usually frequent the upper strata of the aquarium.

Another group, the cichlids, accounts for over 1,000 species, and many of these are very popular aquarium fishes. Unfortunately, many of these grow too large or are too aggressive to be considered good community tank fishes. Probably the best-known cichlid is the angelfish *(Pterophyllum scalare)*, which is often kept in community aquaria, rightly or wrongly. Angelfish can become quite large, and a species tank of these graceful, cherubic-looking cichlids can be stunning. Discus *(Symphysodon* spp.) are considered by many to be the royalty of the hobby and

The red-lined tetra, *Hemigrammus erythrozonus*.

have countless fans. The only drawback is that they are considered a bit delicate; one really needs to research their care before making such investment.

Invertebrates are optional. Snails are considered indispensable by some, a nuisance by others. Give credit where credit is due, though. They are tireless scavengers and are interesting in their own right. Some other "critters" that are often sold in pet shops are crayfish and ghost shrimp, endearing and amusing.

Some Selected Fishes

Is there an aquarist who doesn't have a favorite fish? I doubt it. The following accounts will introduce you to some of my favorites that I hope will become yours also. But I won't tell you what my real favorite is...

Paracheirodon axelrodi, the cardinal tetra, is a brilliant neon-colored fish found in forest pools in Brazil. It grows to about 2 inches and is happiest when kept in schools of seven or more fish. The water should be clear, neutral to slightly acid, and moderately soft. Temperature 70 to 80°F. Plants are beneficial to the well-being of these fish. They are peaceful. Egglayers. Feed on small live food and good dry food; frozen and freeze-dried

The brilliantly colored cardinal tetra, *Paracheirodon axelrodi*.

foods are also appreciated.

Hemigrammus rhodostomus, the rummy-nose tetra, is a pretty little fish, peaceful and active; maximum size, 2 inches. Also from the Amazon region, they like a warm tank not below 79°F or their red noses will fade. Soft, neutral to slightly acid water. They are egglayers. Rummy-noses feed well on dried, live, and frozen foods.

Hyphessobrycon bentosi, the rosy tetra, is a lovely fish, also from the Amazon region. Soft, slightly acid water preferred with temperatures of 75 to 81°F. Egglayer. Thrives on dried, live, or frozen foods. Prefers sinking or moving food. This is a very classy fish and grows to about 2 inches.

Hyphessobrycon pulchripinnis, the lemon tetra, comes from the Amazon basin. This very attractive schooling fish will occupy the mid and lower strata of your community aquarium. Very peaceful. Well-planted, moderately bright aquaria with neutral water. Prefers sinking or moving food. Egglayer. Grows to 2 inches.

Gasteropelecus sternicla, the silver hatchetfish from South America, is long-lived, hardy, and unusual to look at. These fish must be kept in covered aquaria. They occupy the upper level of the tank. They grow to about 2.5 to 3 inches. They really need some live food, even small cockroaches. The water should be soft and slightly acid. Temperature 72 to 82°F. They are egglayers, but little is known about their breeding habits.

Puntius conchonius, the rosy barb, is from India and Bengal. They live in rivers, streams, ditches…moving water. They

grows to about 2 inches. They are best kept in a school and are good community fish. Water conditions are not critical. Aeration is recommended. 70 to 80°F. Will take most small fish foods well.

Brachydanio rerio, the zebra danio, from Bengal and eastern India, grows to 2 inches and is also an excellent community fish. Keep the tank covered, they are leapers! Water conditions are not critical. Temperatures in the range of 65 to 80°F. Accepts all small fish foods.

are easily maintained and undemanding. They are best kept in small schools in roomy, well-planted aquariums. Temperature 65 to 85°F. Good beginner fish. They are egglayers and grow to 3 to 4 inches.

Capoeta tetrazona, the tiger barb, from Borneo and Sumatra, is best kept in groups in well-planted, bright, well-aerated aquaria. They are a little nippy, but not too bad when kept in a group. Neutral, not too hard water with temperature in the 72 to 80°F range. Varied diet. Egglayer.

Brachydanio albolineatus is from India and Sumatra. Commonly called the pearl danio, this lovely fish

31

They are omnivorous. They are seldom-bred egglayers.

Rasbora heteromorpha, the harlequin rasbora, is Asian and tiny, less than one inch in length. It is best kept with other small, peaceful fishes in heavily planted tanks. Keep in schools. Water should be soft and acid. Small live foods are preferred.

Tanichthys albonubes, White Cloud Mountain minnow, is from China. This is an excellent community fish, hardy and undemanding. Accepts a very wide range of water conditions and temperatures. Grows to about 1.5 inches and takes almost any small food. They are egglayers and very easily bred.

Acanthophthalmus kuhlii, the coolie loach, is also from the Orient. They will attain a length of about 4 inches. Prefers heavily planted aquaria. This fish is an egg laying bottom feeder.

Labeo bicolor, the red-tailed shark, is from Thailand and is a gorgeous, robust fish. They can grow to 5 or 6 inches, but not usually. They are usually peaceful with other fishes, but get nasty with each other, so one to a tank, please. The water should be moderately soft to medium-hard and within a few degrees of neutral in either direction. Temperature in the 72 to 80°F range.

Botia macracantha the clown loach, is from Borneo and Sumatra. A truly brilliant fish that will

ttain a length of about 5
nches.   Keep in a larger
quarium with plants and rocks
nd you will see why they have
he common name "clown
oach." Water should be
moderately soft and neutral to
omewhat acid. Temperature in
he range of 72 to 80°F.
Omnivorous. Never bred in the
quarium. Note: Small clown
oaches require frequent
eedings of live foods, tubifex
referred, for about the first two
veeks in the aquarium to get
tarted. Many small clown
oaches are needlessly lost
ecause an unwary aquarist is
ot familiar with this
equirement. They are *well
orth the effort!*

Corydoras aeneus, the bronze
orydoras, is from South
merica and grows to 3 inches.

The black molly,
Poecilia sphenops.

They are good community fish
and will help keep the substrate
cleared. Water conditions are
not critical. Egglayers.
Omnivorous.

Poecilia sphenops, the black
molly, is from the southern U.S.
and Mexico. They prefer
slightly hard, alkaline water
with some salt (about 1
teaspoon per gallon). Warm

The clown loach,
Botia macracantha.

33

The sailfin molly, *Poecilia velifera*.

foods. Excellent growth with live brine shrimp added to the diet.

Poecilia velifera, the green sailfin molly, can grow to 5 inches. A livebearer, it benefits from 1 or 2 teaspoons of salt per gallon of water. Large, well-planted aquaria with somewhat hard and alkaline water are best. Don't overcrowd. Needs some vegetation and will eat most aquarium foods.

Xiphophorus helleri, the swordtail, comes from Central

The sailfin molly, *Poecilia velifera*.

water, about 75 to 80°F, a little sunlight, some vegetable foods, and you will have a hard time controlling the population of this beautiful livebearer.

The swordtail, *Xiphophorus helleri*.

Poecilia reticulata, the guppy, is probably the world's best-known fish. Excellent with other very small fishes. They grow to about 1.5 to 2 inches. Tolerates temperatures in the 65 to 85°F range, but sensitive to chilling. A very prolific livebearer that accepts a wide range of

America. The swordtail grows to about 4 inches and should be kept covered. Will take all aquarium foods with some vegetable food. Moderately hard, alkaline water preferred.

The platy, *Xiphophorus maculatus*.

A prolific, easy-to-breed livebearer.

Xiphophorus maculatus, the platy, is from Central America and is recommended to all new aquarists. It is an excellent, undemanding, peaceful aquarium fish that grows to the respectable size of about 3 inches. A prolific livebearer, the platy will take all aquarium foods, but benefits from some vegetable foods.

Trichogaster leeri, the pearl or lace gourami, is a super good-looking anabantoid. A bubble-nest builder, the pearl gourami is cited as one of the most elegant and beautiful of all freshwater tropical fishes. Attaining about 4 inches at maturity, this is a fish with a preference for small worms, but is not fussy and will accept all aquarium foods. Temperatures of 75 to 80°F are ideal.

Betta splendens, the Siamese fighting fish, is from Asia. It grows to about 2.5 inches. Bubble-nest builder. Water

Betta splendens. The betta is renowned worldwide for its beauty and courage. The flaring gills on one of the fish in this photo indicate that unless these males are separated, they will start fighting any moment. Male bettas even display hostility to their own images in the tank glass.

conditions are not critical except for warmth. Keep males separate! Omnivorous.

Colisa sota, the honey gourami, is from India and Assam. They grow to about 2 inches. Warm water, about 75 to 82°F and other conditions not critical. Shy and peaceful, this fish prefers a planted aquarium. Bubblenest builder, this fish prefers high quality live, frozen, or dried foods.

Astronotus ocellatus, the oscar, is a very popular cichlid from South America. This fish can only be kept in a large aquarium, at least 40 gallons, as it can reach 12 inches in length and has a very bulky body. The oscar is famous for its "intelligence" and "personality" and can be taught to take food from your fingers. Oscars will eat most foods, prefer large pieces, and will make short work of feeder fish. Egglayer.

Cichlasoma meeki is a very beautiful cichlid that gets along will with most fishes that don't give it a hard time. It stays within reasonable size, so a pair can be housed in a 20-gallon tank without difficulty. They will eat live, frozen, and prepared foods.

INTRODUCING THE FISHES

When you first set up your tank you will want to stock lightly. Even though some

fishes are nearly irresistible, it is wise to avoid buying all the fishes you plan for your aquarium at once. It's best to stay with the smaller specimens at first. If, for example, you have decided you want ten cardinal tetras, eight black neon tetras, eight lemon tetras, four rosy barbs, two gold barbs, six zebra danios, two corydoras, two hatchetfish, and four platies in a 40-gallon tank, you could start with the smaller schooling fish and just buy your school of cardinal tetras first. Let the tank and the fish relax for a week. If everything is going well, add the neon tetras; then let the tank relax again. Then proceed on with your fish purchases.

There are several good reasons for this gradual stocking

of the tank. When you spread your fish purchases over several weeks, it gives you time to really look at the specimens that are being offered for sale. An impulse purchase often brings headaches. Perhaps the platies are a little threadbare this week; how disappointed you would be if there is a great new color form and big, healthy fish the next week! Or vice versa. Suppose you planned to buy the corys this week but something else looked great. If you bought all your fish at once, you would be subject to whatever happened to be in the store on that particular day and could well miss out on the bargain of a lifetime with the next shipment the dealer received. The tank itself also needs the time to adjust. While your lovely school of cardinal tetras may seem a bit lost in the tank

It's great fun to go to the pet shop and select your new fishes!

When selecting specimens for your new tank, try to get the most healthy looking individuals available. Avoid fish with white spots, clamped fins.

Slowly add tank water to the water in the transport bag.

at first, you know they will soon have companions and it is just a matter of a short time before the water ages and the nitrogen cycle is established.

Overloading an uncycled tank is the biggest mistake a newcomer can make. The water is just too pure to handle the leftover food and waste of more than a few fishes at a time. Also, it is just possible that something is not

fish arrived in. Then you can gently net your fish and introduce them to your tank. This method gives the fish a chance to adjust to your water and temperature and reduces the chance of disease carried by strange water. They may be a little stunned at first, but will soon begin to explore their new home. Wait a few hours before feeding, until you feel they are used to the tank, or else they won't eat and the food will go to waste, possibly starting a nasty water quality problem.

Release fish and water into a holding container; slowly add more water from your tank until you have approximately half tank water and half original water in the container. Then net the fish and introduce it to your aquarium.

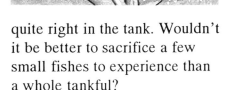

quite right in the tank. Wouldn't it be better to sacrifice a few small fishes to experience than a whole tankful?

When you get the fish home, empty the fish and water into a clean (soap-free) container. Gently add a small amount of water from your tank. Wait 10 to 15 minutes and add some more tank water. Do this until you have doubled the water the

Try to equalize the temperature of the waters before you add the fish to your aquarium. A drastic temperature change is very harmful to fish.

FEEDING YOUR FISHES

At mealtime there are only three types of fishes—carnivores (meat-eaters), herbivores (vegetarians), and omnivores, which dine on both meat and vegetable matter. We often find that herbivores that eat only vegetable matter in the wild will often "cross over" in the aquarium and feast on live worms and brine shrimp, so use the term "herbivore" as an indication that these fishes require vegetable matter for health, but not exclusively. *Poecilia*, *Xiphophorus*, and *Pseudotropheus* species are but a few of the fishes that are omnivorous.

There are many carnivorous species. The term carnivorous in fishes can mean anything from true meat-eaters like piranhas, that attack and devour anything from hapless bovines and other meaty foods, to fishes that are well satisfied with small worms and other insects.

There are many different kinds of food sold in pet shops that will be good for your fishes. Prepared foods are scientifically developed to provide the nutrients necessary

Brine shrimp, *Artemia salina*, are highly recommended for conditioning your fishes. Rinse the brine shrimp to remove residual salt before introducing them into your aquarium.

to keep your fishes healthy. These foods are wholesome and acceptable to most fishes. Still, there are different kinds of foods. A carnivorous fish would probably adapt and eat a diet high in vegetable matter out of desperation, but this fish would not be in the peak of health, color, or reproductive ability.

Feeding your fishes is probably almost as much fun for you as it is for them. Fish food is not expensive and should not be the target of any budget cuts. When selecting the food for your fishes, make sure the particles are of the correct size. There are prepared foods available in every size from the finest fry food to huge pellets for cichlids and pond fish. One huge pellet will probably be ignored by starving guppies. By the same token, feeding a fine flake food to a large oscar wouldn't offer much satisfaction to this fish.

Variety is very important. Even the most delicious meal would quickly become unpleasant if served all the time. It is not just that the palate will become bored, but the nutritional integrity of the diet would not be adequate. The same holds true in the aquarium.

The quantity of food offered must be judicious. Do not feed more than the fishes will consume in five minutes. Feeding three times a day is not too frequent. Small, frequent feedings are much more efficient than trying to give the ration all at once. Do not be fooled—most fish look hungry all the time. It's a trick. If you cover the surface of the water with food, you will soon see that most of the food will end up in the gravel. When food sits in the gravel in a heated aquarium for even a short period, it will decay. This decaying food will ruin your water quality in no time. So you must gauge how much food to give depending upon the size and number of your fishes. Experience will be your best teacher in the quantity of food to offer your fishes. There is a relationship between water temperature and the feeding habits of tropical fishes. Tropicals will typically require more food if kept in warmer temperatures and brighter light.

Be sure that the majority of the food is not consumed by a bully in the tank. It is not uncommon that a dominant fish will know where you habitually drop the food and select that site as his exclusive territory, allowing the others only the

upper photo: Todays aquarium hobbyists have a very wide range of commercially prepared foods available to them for feeding their fish. Among the most popular are the flake foods. Photo courtesy of Wardley.

lower photo: For the traveling aquarist multiple-day feeders are available. They provide a convenient way of properly feeding your fish. Photo courtesy of Aquarium Pharmaceuticals, Inc.

remnants that float out of his area. If you see that this is happening, vary your feeding site or put small amounts in each corner of the tank. This will allow less assertive fishes to get their fair share.

There are fishes that are nocturnal feeders and arrangements must be made for them also. *Notopterus chitala,* the clown knifefish, is one such fish. The technique with these fish is to turn off the light and feed. If you want to make sure they are eating, use a flashlight or watch them with a subdued room light in the evening. You will soon find that they are just as hungry as any other fish!

As you have probably deduced from the previous paragraphs, flake and pelleted food are not the only available choices. There are many different kinds of food you can feed your fishes, and it is desirable to offer several kinds in rotation. Freeze-dried and frozen foods are very easy to use and are available year 'round in most places. Live foods will tempt even reluctant feeders. If you think about it, fish in their native habitat do not feed on neat, round pellets of combined nutrients. They browse their environs for anything that looks tasty. Fish like to eat insects, small fishes, algae, and plants.

Many professional aquarists believe that anything less than live food simply will not do. They keep cultures of mosquito larvae going in the basement at all times; they may also keep another box with worms reproducing. This is not quite practical for most of us with one or even a few aquaria. But the fundamental belief is still valid. There is no food like live, moving insects for conditioning your fishes, be it for spawning or just to keep them in optimal health and vitality.

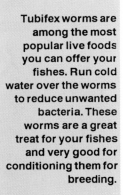

Tubifex worms are among the most popular live foods you can offer your fishes. Run cold water over the worms to reduce unwanted bacteria. These worms are a great treat for your fishes and very good for conditioning them for breeding.

Live foods are sold in your pet shops. Understandably, all shops do not keep their selection of worms out on the counter. Ask and ye shall find! In many areas the availability of live foods varies according to season, but you will always be able to provide live food either by means of directly purchasing from your pet shop or from simple cultures you can maintain in your own home.

Live Foods

Brine shrimp (*Artemia salina*) is a wonderful food that is incredibly easy to hatch in the home. The amazing thing about the eggs of this creature is that they can be dried and kept indefinitely. Even the smallest fishes will readily accept newly hatched brine shrimp. Brine shrimp eggs and the instructions for their culture are available at virtually every pet shop regardless of season. Frozen brine shrimp is available in two sizes: adult and newly hatched. The adult size is good for medium and larger-sized fishes. The newly hatched brine shrimp are good for smaller fishes and fry, but be aware that since they are not alive they will sink to the bottom and leftovers will

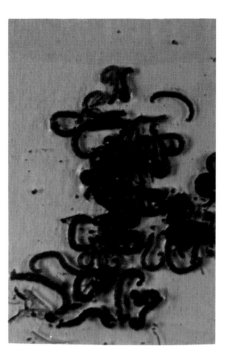

Bloodworms are eagerly eaten by most fishes. Bloodworms are very valuable for enticing difficult fishes to start feeding.

foul the water. Freeze dried brine shrimp float for a while, allowing top and middle strata feeders ample opportunity to get their share.

Tubifex worms, glassworms, bloodworms, and mosquito larvae are but a few of the great live foods your fishes will devour with gusto. There are also vitamins available for fish at the pet shop and it may be that your fishes would benefit from some supplemental feeding with these, especially at times when live foods are in short supply.

Depending upon the population of your tank, a 10 to 25% water change weekly is the act of good aquarist. When you remove this old water and replace it with fresh, conditioned water you are giving your fishes a new lease on life. Changing a portion of the water on a gradual, routine basis will insure against toxic levels of nitrate and ammonia and help the filter in its job.

The maintenance of your tank should be a pleasure, not a burden. Before you start, gather your materials. You will need a bucket (a plastic pail is best) and reserve this for your hobby. Never use a pail that has contained detergents or chemicals. Collect your filter supplies, an algae scraper and soft cloth to clean the outside of the glass. You also need some kind of siphon. Airline tubing is adequate but a bit slow. There are great vacuum devices available to assist in removing the detritus from the gravel at the same time you are siphoning the water. With one of these "gravel washers," as they are called, the removal of 10, 20, or

even 50 gallons of water takes only a matter of minutes.

The gravel washer consists of a tube with a fairly thick hose

attached. When the tube is stuck down in the gravel, the siphon action lifts and swirls the gravel and water in the tube, filtering the water and dirt out through the hose and leaving the gravel behind. Before siphoning the water, stir the gravel gently and see just how dirty the tank really is. If you can stir your gravel and not raise a cloud of dirt, just change some of the water and leave the gravel alone. Gently, though—there's nothing to be gained in overexciting your fishes. When you replace the water you've removed, make every effort to ensure that it is of a temperature similar to that of the tank water. To dump a couple of gallons of icy water in a tank is just asking for trouble.

After the water has been changed, check the filter. Are all the moving parts clear of debris and plant material? Usually if the filter media is gray or dark brown it's time to change it. Don't be too quick about wanting to change the filter material, though. In a new aquarium it could be a month or more before this needs to be done. This is a critical period because the bacteria are just establishing and need to be left alone for a while. Of course, if the media is very soiled, change it.

The inside glass can be cleaned either with a piece of plastic mesh or an algae scraper, but usually it takes some time before this needs to be done. A new tank isn't going to have any algae for a while. The outside of the glass is easily kept clean with a soft cloth. Don't use ammonia or window cleaner! The fumes are dangerous to small animals.

Check your fish. Look for torn fins or harassed fish. Note anything amiss, erratic behavior or unusual spots. Part of successful fishkeeping is

nipping problems in the bud and forestalling massive "die-offs" by early containment of epidemics. If a fish is obviously on his way out, you wouldn't want to keep him in the tank with healthy fish.

If you have been doing your regular weekly maintenance, your aquarium should stay clean and fresh all of the time. Once a month, set aside some time and give your filter a good cleaning. Check your airlines and hoses, plugs and all moving parts to forestall any potential troubles.

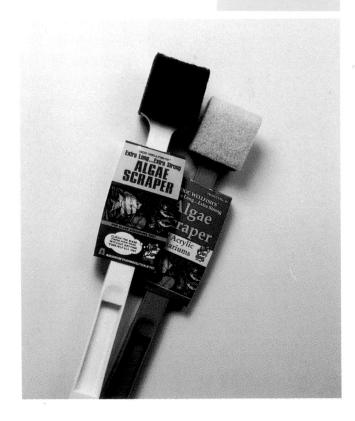

Algae-removing wands are available for both glass and plastic aquaria; those designed for use in plastic aquaria are less abrasive than those used in glass aquaria. Photo courtesy of Aquarium Pharmaceuticals, Inc.

PLANTS IN YOUR AQUARIUM

Your aquarium can have lush plants just like this one! Given time, proper lighting, and fertilization, plants will thrive and grow.

It is interesting to learn that it was actually the cultivation of aquatic plants that gave rise to the hobby of keeping fishes in aquaria. Early botanists learned that their water plant specimens fared better and were more interesting to observe when a few native fishes were added to the aquarium. Thus was conceived the notion of keeping fishes in tanks (in the West anyway; Orientals have been keeping goldfish and koi for centuries). Out of the study of water plants grew an immensely popular pastime that has captivated people from all walks of life.

There are quite literally hundreds of varieties of plants that can be included in your

tropical aquarium. We want our aquariums to look natural, and there is no more satisfying way to achieve this objective than by the cultivation of an underwater garden. Anyone can have healthy greenery in their aquarium if they follow a few simple steps.

First of all, timing is critical. It is obvious to those of us who have tried and failed, that nothing much is going to grow in a new tank. Only plastic plants will survive in a recently set up tank. That is a fact. There simply are not enough nutrients in the substrate to properly feed any but the simplest forms of plant life. You will find that even algae does not grow in a brand new tank. Actually, one of the first signs that your aquarium is approaching "plant ready" could be the appearance of algae, indicating that water is starting to get into condition to support plant life. Plants require nutrients just like any other form of life. The basic source of this nourishment is the mineral-rich waste products of the fishes themselves, which have decomposed in otherwise clean water.

Even after your aquarium has been established for a few weeks don't expect the substrate to contain enough "fish fertilizer" to support more than an algae bloom. One way to circumvent part of the waiting period is to purchase pre-potted plants that already contain a built-in food supply adequate for a few months while waiting for the fishes and bacteria to do their job.

Lighting is just as important to aquatic plants as it is to the roses that so love the sunny spots in our gardens. The tricky part here is that we do not ever place our aquariums in sunlight. This may seem foolish since the plants need light to photosynthesize, and the fishes probably wouldn't mind basking in the afternoon sun, but we would lose too much control over temperature and algae growth— so rule out a southern exposure for your aquarium. What we want to do is use that fluorescent gro-light we just bought with the tank cover. Imitating the natural spectrum of light with a fluorescent strip will provide all the light most plants will need.

Tropical plants naturally occur in waters that are consistently exposed to direct sunlight for 12 hours a day. That is why it is so critical for us to keep the fluorescent light on for 12 to 14 hours a day. Too short a duration of light and the plants absolutely will not make it. A

"Lighting is just as important to aquatic plants as it is to the roses that so love the sunny spots in our gardens."

47

This *Echinodorus* is a lovely plant from the Amazon and quite hardy as well.

timer can be your plant's best friend. This will regulate the duration of exposure and ensure that the light is on at the same time every day which gives the plants a normal light/dark cycle. The day/night rhythm simulated by light and darkness can be seen in the "sleep" condition of some water plants and demonstrates the need for regularity.

Keep the light strip clean because easily 50% of the light intensity can be lost when the tube is encrusted with dust or mineral deposits. There is also a loss of light intensity that normally occurs as the fluorescent tube ages that is not easily discerned; so it wouldn't be

wasteful after a year to replace a tube that hadn't yet burned out.

Most tropical plants will do quite well in the same water as your fishes. The one concession you could make to their comfort without compromising the animal life is to raise the temperature a little. Plants do not do well if their roots are chilled; bear this in mind and adjust the temperature to the upper limits for your fishes.

It is not easy for the novice to know which plants to select for his aquarium. On what basis should the selection be made? Do we buy the plant that appeals to our esthetic sense, or buy on price alone? The answer is both. Your pet shop will have a selection of plants that are both pleasing to the eye and the wallet.

Give yourself a head start on your botanical success and only purchase healthy, vigorous plants. Aquarium plants can be classified in three main groups and there are different standards to look for in each group.

The first type to consider are the floating plants. They draw their sustenance directly from the water and should not be anchored to the substrate or gravel. Choose specimens that are crisp and green with healthy root systems. The more tiny,

hair-like roots, the better. The leaves should be green and healthy looking. Avoid a plant that has mushy or yellowing leaves. In addition to adding a unique finishing touch to your aquarium, they provide a fine spawning site for bubblenest-builders like bettas and gouramis and offer additional cover for tiny fry. These floating plants will enhance the purity of your water because they do not rely on the gravel bed for their nourishment and utilize wastes from the water itself. One potential problem is that these plants could easily overwhelm the surface of your aquarium, blocking light to the lower level and interfering with the plants below. So cull these plants when they get out of bounds. About 50% coverage is probably not out of line. Among the most popular and commonly available floating plants are floating water sprite *(Ceratopteris pteroides)*, duckweed *(Lemna minor)*, water lettuce *(Pistia stratiotes)*, floating ferns *(Azolla* spp.), and salvinia *(Salvinia rotundifolia)*.

The next group to include in your established aquarium are the bunch plants—usually these are the culprits that give aquatic plants a bad name. The true villain may actually be the rubber band that holds them together in the bunch. Remove this as soon as you get your

plants home, as it can only lead to rot and ruin. Banded or not, again look for specimens with well-developed roots whenever possible. In any case, reject any plant that is yellowed or breaks easily. These plants are often floated and planted in the gravel when they have developed good roots. The most common of these are *Elodea* species which are often very hardy. *Cabomba,* or fanwort, is a favorite for plant-eating fishes. *Hygrophila* and *Ludwiga* are also very hardy and popular. These bunch plants are prolific and when established grow very quickly.

Fully rooted plants are the third basic type and are the ones most often available in pots (the preferred type for newer aquariums). Good choices in this area would be full-looking plants with many leaves and evidence of new growth. Sometimes you will run across a plant that has suffered much and has little top growth. If you must have this specimen, let the condition of the roots be the deciding factor. If there's a good strong root system and the top growth is weak, chances are the plant will recover and present you with equally healthy leaves in a very short time. There are many species to choose from, some of the more popular being swordplants *(Echinodorus* spp.), arrowheads, *(Sagittaria* spp.), and eel grass *(Vallisneria* spp.).

When planting your new specimens, be careful not to break off any more of the roots than possible. Remove any damaged or yellow leaves.

Rinse the plant in tepid water to minimize the possibility of introducing unwanted guests (snails) to your aquarium. It is sometimes difficult to anchor your plants well, but your pet shop offers lead anchors that can help, especially if you have gravel-digging fishes that love to uproot plants. Only if the plant is allowed to remain in the

same spot will it be able to send out the roots that will hold it in position in the gravel. Be careful when doing your maintenance that you don't disturb the roots of the plants.

Part of the beauty of an aquarium is the variety of life that can be found within. Keep your eyes open and you will find many different plants in

your dealer's tanks. Don't try to plant the aquarium all in one day. What might be a good selection of plants on any given day may be surpassed by the next delivery from the wholesaler. And remember, slowly—you want your plants to grow and look beautiful, not starve to death in a tank that just isn't established enough to support their needs.

Top: Avoid plants with rotting leaves and weak roots.

Center: Rinse new plants in tepid water to remove any unwanted snails.

Bottom: Bury the roots in the soil, but avoid breaking the roots during planting. Potted plants should also be planted in the gravel. There is no need to remove the pot.

Part of the proof of your success in aquarium management comes when your fish decide to reproduce. Aquarium hobby magazines and books are largely dedicated to reports of breeding fishes, as well as finding them and keeping them, but to breed a new or difficult species is considered the pinnacle of success.

Fortunately, the fishes that have been in the hobby for a while are usually most cooperative and will willingly spawn in your aquarium. Provided they have the correct conditions and you know what to do to save the fry, you could have more fish than you know what to do with in no time at all.

Unlike most mammals that

take quite a while to produce their young, fish eggs can hatch in a matter of hours—even the livebearers that carry the fry in their ovaries and deliver self-sufficient young produce fry quickly and regularly. However, the mortality rate of the young fish is quite high, so it's not likely that the situation will get out of hand. Even if you do save and raise more fry than you can accommodate, there is usually a friend or friendly pet shop that will happily take them off your hands.

There are egglayers and livebearers. Livebearers are probably the easiest for the beginner to breed. Aside from providing the parent fish with good food and good water quality, the only other thing you have to do is protect the offspring from their parents and the other fish in the tank. Livebearers are from the family Poecilidae, the guppies, mollies, swordtails, platies, limias, and more.

Egglayers are a bit more challenging. To breed egglayers, you must provide the same conditions as for livebearers—good food, good water—but you must also protect the eggs and provide for their specific needs,

Marigold swordtails, *Xiphophorus helleri*. These excellent specimens will produce many, many fry. The goal of a breeding program with fish of this quality is to produce fry equal to the parent fish. The male is the fish with the swordtail and he was approaching one of the females even as the photo was taken.

This is a pair of guppies, *Poecilia reticulata*. The female is much larger than the male, but the male is much more colorful than the female. It is very easy to sex guppies, so you should have no trouble finding a pair to establish your breeding colony.

and then raise the fry. Breeding egglayers is by no means impossible, or even difficult in many cases; there are just different criteria.

Livebearers

In livebearing fishes, the male is usually the more colorful and possesses an intromittent organ called a gonopodium that is an elongated, partially fused anal fin. Young fish and females have the typical rounded anal fin. If you have doubts, your pet shop can usually tell the difference and see to it that you get a pair.

The fish you choose to breed must be young and healthy. Do not breed immature fish or old fish. An immature fish will not produce good fry, nor will she develop properly herself. So when you breed immature females, you are reversing the progress that has already been made with this strain and

producing small, underdeveloped fish. Your chances of having a spawn worth saving are dramatically increased if the fish are in tip-top condition.

The pre-spawning diet is very important. Special feeding is called "conditioning." This is necessary if you wish to have worthwhile spawn. Doubtless the fish will go ahead and breed without special treatment, but remember, the goal here is a worthwhile spawn that you will be proud to show your friends. It would be very disheartening to go to the trouble to save fry and end up with misshapen, puny fish. To condition your fish well, feed often and with quality live foods for about two weeks. You will be able to see the difference. They will be robust and full of vitality. This is the kind of fish you want to reproduce.

During the conditioning

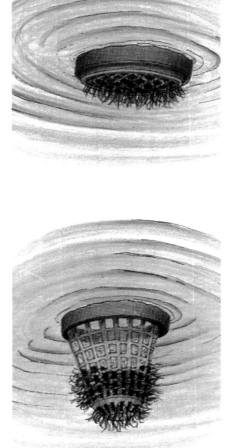

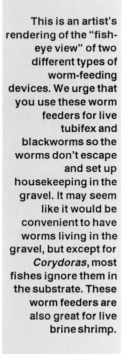

This is an artist's rendering of the "fish-eye view" of two different types of worm-feeding devices. We urge that you use these worm feeders for live tubifex and blackworms so the worms don't escape and set up housekeeping in the gravel. It may seem like it would be convenient to have worms living in the gravel, but except for *Corydoras*, most fishes ignore them in the substrate. These worm feeders are also great for live brine shrimp.

Another facet of the conditioning of your breeders is light and warmth. Gestation time is reduced in bright light. By the same token, a warmer tank, in the upper range of ideal temperatures, will help bring the embryos to maturity faster.

One distinction with livebearers that is not necessarily true of all egglayers is that they are cannibals. There is no kind of parental care involved. The female fish will drop the fry and then turn a round and immediately eat them! Except for some egglayers that care for their young, it's open season for fry at any time in the aquarium, especially in the community tank. Of course, the chances of saving fry are immeasurably enhanced if the mother has been conditioned and well-fed. Undoubtedly there will be many pregnancies, even in the community aquarium, but the chances of saving even part of the spawn are just about nil unless you are very lightly stocked with fish, have a lot of (plants, rocks, and other nooks and crannies inaccessible to ravenous relatives in pursuit of fry), and feed the adults well.

The prospect of raising fry in a community tank is an interesting one to ponder. You

period it is best to keep the sexes separate. You don't want any accidents. It is almost impossible to keep some fishes from becoming pregnant, however. Many livebearers are pregnant even in the dealer's tanks. Also, don't be surprised if you find your female guppy pregnant and there is no male around. This is not a miracle. As many as eight pregnancies have been recorded from one copulation with these fish!

will truly see the difficulties presented to the young of fish and almost every other animal in nature. It is an almighty wonder that any of these creatures survive at all. These hardy little fellows pop right out of the womb (well, not exactly, a fish doesn't have a uterus; the fry are carried in the ovary) and immediately have to run for their lives!

To insure that our fry have the very best chances for survival, there are certain things we will do for them. First, we will choose the very best pair we can find, or better yet, a half dozen very similar fish. We will condition them well. They will be healthy. They will have the best water conditions. They will have warmth and light. There

The Java moss, *Vesicularia*, growing in this tank will provide excellent cover for fry.

will be enough room in the tank to raise them comfortably. In return for all this care and devotion, their fry will grow up into beautiful fish that you can be proud of.

Unless you have been boning up on fish genetics, do not attempt to mix and match your breeding pair. Only breed the best two fish that look alike, whether wild-caught or commercially developed. If you are breeding similar fish, your chances of having a good spawn are that much better. Try fooling around with Mother Nature and you will probably get garbage. It might seem that crossing the red-tail guppy and a blue-tail guppy will produce nice babies, but believe me, the result will not be a purple-tail guppy of the same quality as the parents.

There are several ways to breed livebearers depending upon the amount of control you

This female guppy is preparing to make a fast snack of her newborn fry.

55

wish to exert over the selection of the parents. One way is to leave the parent fish in the community and let nature take her course. Then remove the fry as you can. You may get some nice fish from each spawn; but considering the amount of effort involved in raising the spawn, is it worth it? If you want to keep a goodly number of the fry, try using breeding traps that float in the community tank. As soon as you see the gravid spot on the female, capture her and put her in the trap. When she delivers her fry, release her into the main tank and save the fry. I have some problems with this method. First, if the trap holds two cups of water, it's a lot, and the water gets very foul in the trap unless you dump it daily. Then you must capture a gestating fish, which could lead to miscarriage, and will certainly cause stress. And yes, this method does work fairly well, but the method of choice is a breeding tank.

The Breeding Tank For Livebearers

A breeding tank should be of adequate size for the fish you wish to spawn. A 10-gallon tank is quite large enough for the

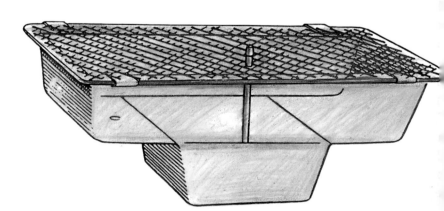

small livebearing fishes. Too large a tank will result in the fry getting lost and not being able to find food. Use plenty of live plants, as these will provide cover for the newborns and give them the security they need. The best plants for shelter are Java moss, *Myriophyllum,* and *Salvinia,* but any bushy plant will do the job.

Provide the best quality water you can. I half fill the tank with water from the community tank and half new (dechlorinated) water. Don't forget that this tank needs some time to cycle as with any new tank; but since you have some water from the established tank and are not trying to overstock it with fish, it should be safe within one or two days. If your substrate is thick in the community tank, you can take some of the used gravel from there and use it for your breeding tank. This will help prevent "new tank syndrome." The only time to use the gravel and water from the established tank, of course, is if you are very sure that your tank is healthy—no disease or recent mortalities. The best type of filter to use in a tank with fry is a very simple sponge filter that they can't get sucked up into. A pump attached to the filter and airstone by a gang-valve will

take care of your filtration and aeration needs. A heater, thermometer, and fluorescent light will complete your equipment needs.

After this tank has been operative for a couple of days, select your female(s) and introduce them to the new tank. Use the same method as with any new fish, gently mixing water from the two tanks to acclimate the fish. Then release them into the tank. Leave the lights low for a few hours to give them time to relax. Fish, as you know by now, are susceptible to stress. So take it easy. Set up the breeding tank away from busy areas of the home.

After your fish have settled down a bit and appear relaxed in their new home you can feed very lightly. Very small amounts, often, and of high quality live foods are the best for conditioning your breeding stock. With livebearers, the fish and their appetites are so small

It is not difficult to set up a tank for fry. Light, warmth, clean water, and good food are all that are required to raise your fry into healthy adult fish.

that it's not in any way prohibitive financially to serve them the very best. Just be careful not to overfeed. You wouldn't want to end up with toxic water conditions at this stage of the game.

After a few days of this conditioning—good food, warm, clean water, and a new fluorescent tube lit for 12 hours a day—introduce your male(s) and continue the same regimen of conditioning.

Hopefully your female will not have been already expecting and the male you chose will be the father. I don't know that there are any guarantees of this unless the sexes have been segregated since infancy. As mentioned before, female livebearers can have many spawns from just one sex act. The sperm is stored in the ovary for a long time and fertilizes

eggs time after time. However, for the sake of argument, we will assume the fish you chose are to be the parent fish. In any event, with livebearers, the male will not care if the female is pregnant or not so you will still be able to observe the courtship ritual, which will take place almost immediately.

Whether you have chosen to breed a single pair or a dozen similar fish, the female(s) will soon develop a noticeable gravid spot behind the anal fin. This is proof of pregnancy. This is a good time to remove the male(s) to avoid their harassing the mother(s). Continue your good feedings and remember to keep the temperature level at about 82°F. Within about 28 days there should be fry everywhere. As soon as you see that the female has dropped her young, get her out of there! Even

This guppy is giving birth to her live fry. The baby is coiled in a ball at birth, and within seconds straightens out and swims away. A female guppy could easily produce 30 fry at one time.

hough you have fed her well and have plenty of cover for the fry, she is absolutely not to be trusted not to cannibalize her young.

At this stage, the fry are little more than eyes carrying around translucent slivers of body, but they are large compared to most egglayer fry. They will take fry food readily. Very finely chopped tubifex, microworms, and newly hatched brine shrimp give the fry a critical head start. Again, feed often and well. Keep the temperature in the fry tank at 82°F and institute small, frequent water changes as much of the food will be wasted and foul the water.

Egglayers

There are many variations in the spawning habits of the different kinds of egglayers.

There are fishes that scatter their eggs, some that build bubblenests, some that carry their eggs around in their mouths, and more... To describe the methods of each of the

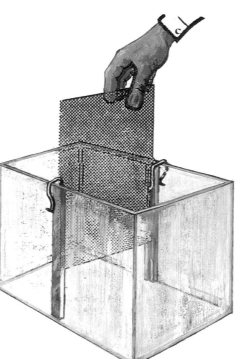

egglayer types would fill volumes (and has).

Egg scatterers are perhaps the easiest of the groups to spawn and include the majority of aquarium fishes. Some of the egg scatterers lay adhesive eggs that stick to plants and the glass of the aquarium; with others, the eggs fall to the bottom.

Unfortunately, nearly all of the egglayers will eat their eggs if given the opportunity. So again, you must protect the spawn from their parents and other fishes in the tank.

It is possible to discern sexual differences among the egglayers. The male is usually smaller and more brightly colored. The female will become more obvious as she fills with roe. Usually, the female is a little stouter, larger, and less colorful. Some of these fish have differently colored sexes.

As with the livebearers, it is necessary to condition the fishes first. It cannot be said with enough emphasis how valuable conditioning is to the production of a good spawn. Well-fed parents produce more eggs and that improves the odds when it comes to having a good number of fry reach maturity. Remember that in nature, a pair of fish is considered successful if just two of their offspring live long enough to mature and

reproduce. That's pretty awesome when you consider how many eggs are laid by a given pair in their lifetime.

When preparing a breeding tank for egg scatterers like the danios (*Brachydanio* spp.) and tetras (*Hyphessobrycon* and *Hemigrammus* spp.), it is best to include many plants. The bottoms of the breeding tanks for egglayers are often covered with marbles, which help prevent the parents from eating the eggs. The eggs drop between the marbles where the parents can't get to them. A combination of plants and marbles will insure that you

protect most of the eggs from the parents.

Our example is the famous

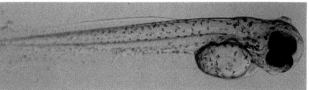

egg scatterer *Brachydanio rerio*, the zebra danio. A most hardy fish, the zebra danio will endure a wide range of water conditions and temperatures, but for a

Top: This colony of *Hemigrammus pulcher* will produce many eggs in the breeding tank. You will be able to save most of the fry if you have plenty of fine-leaved plants for protection.

Center: This newly-hatched *Hemigrammus rhodostomus* is still living off its yolk sac.

Bottom: A pair of well-conditioned zebra danios. The female is obviously swollen with eggs.

61

breeding tank, the water should be close to neutral, moderately hard, and 76 to 78°F.

A very beautiful fish, the zebra danio prefers to be kept in schools. There will be many spawnings in the community tank, but as with most fishes, the eggs and fry are devoured without any chance of making it to adulthood. These fish are incredibly easy to spawn.

In order to breed the zebra danio, select six to nine healthy-looking, mature fish, at least 2 inches in length. They are easy to sex. The female is slightly larger and much deeper-bodied. The male is more slender and usually more colorful. Separate

the sexes and condition them with live foods for a few days.

When the fish are ready to spawn, the males will be bright and active and the females will be noticeably more plump than before. At this time, place them in the prepared breeding tank; 5 or 10 gallons will do nicely. The tank should be well-planted, have a coarse gravel substrate or a layer of dark marbles.

The dawn of the following

day will probably induce spawning activity. The males, in a frenzy, will drive the females through the plants. Side by side, they will quiver spasmodically and the eggs and sperm will be released simultaneously. About 200 eggs will be produced from each female, scattered about the tank wherever they fall. When the spawning is complete, return the adults to the community tank.

In about 24 to 36 hours (depending on temperature), the eggs will hatch. The fry will absorb their nutrient yolk sacs and become free-swimming in about two days. At this point, they will be tiny and transparent. Even at this tender age, the fry will take prepared fry foods, either liquid or finely crushed flake. They grow very quickly, reaching about one inch in only three months if fed properly and often.

Specific breeding accounts are widely available for just

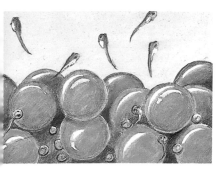

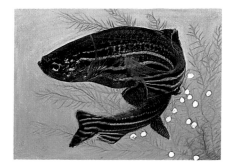

about every ornamental fish in the hobby. Some species have not yet been bred in captivity and, what luck (and skill) if you are the individual to first induce a "tough" species to spawn!

One example is the lovely *Synodontis angelicus*, a gorgeous and costly catfish species from the Congo. Needless to say, there are many people who make their livings at breeding fishes, but there have been many instances where novices have made the discoveries that have stumped the experts. Who knows? You may be the lucky individual that ichthyological history honors. Your fishes don't know if you have a PhD. after your name, and even if they did, they wouldn't care. The fishes "care" about being well fed and being kept in clean and comfortable surroundings.

The male squeezes the eggs from the female and fertilizes them as they are released.

The eggs have incubated in the protected crevices in the substrate.

The angelicus catfish, *Synodontis angelicus*.

INDEX